The Dust Bowl

Revised Edition

An Interactive History Adventure

❋

by Allison Lassieur

CAPSTONE PRESS
a capstone imprint

You Choose Books are published by Capstone Press,
1710 Roe Crest Drive, North Mankato, Minnesota 56003.
www.mycapstone.com

Library of Congress Cataloging-in-Publication Data is available on the Library of Congress website.
978-1-5157-4303-3 (revised hardcover)
978-1-5157-4262-3 (revised paperback)
978-1-5157-4375-0 (eBook pdf)
978-1-5157-4326-2 (eBook)

Editorial Credits
Angie Kaelberer, editor; Juliette Peters, set designer; Gene Bentdahl, book designer;
     Wanda Winch, photo researcher

Photo Credits
AP Photo: 12, 27, 30, 34, 37; Capstone Press: 10; Getty Images: Alfred Eisenstaedt/The LIFE
Picture Collection, 42, Bettmann, 56, 70, Popperfoto, 8; Library of Congress: Cover, 6, 18, 20, 47,
51, 66, 68, 72, 74, 81, 85, 86, 90, 99; Newscom: KANSAS STATE HISTORICAL SOCIETY/
KRT, 77; Shutterstock: Everett Historical, 54, 63, Sari ONea, 102; USDA/NRCS: 17

Capstone Press thanks Dr. James Stuebbendieck, Director, Center for Great Plains Studies,
University of Nebraska–Lincoln, for his assistance with this book.

TABLE OF CONTENTS

ABOUT YOUR ADVENTURE

YOU are living in the United States during the 1930s. The Great Depression has gripped the country, causing people to lose their farms, jobs, and homes. How will you survive?

In this book, you'll explore how the choices people made meant the difference between life and death. The events you'll experience happened to real people.

Chapter One sets the scene. Then you choose which path to read. Follow the directions at the bottom of each page. The choices you make will change your outcome. After you finish one path, go back and read the others for new perspectives and more adventures.

YOU CHOOSE the path
you take through history.

5

In the 1920s, farmers in the Great Plains plowed thousands of acres of land.

From Land to Dust

Long before the first European explorers came, American Indians and the buffalo lived throughout the Great Plains. This wide prairie stretches from Canada all the way south to Texas. It spreads east of the Rocky Mountains to the eastern Dakotas, Nebraska, Kansas, and Oklahoma.

In the mid- to late 1800s, the U.S. government forced American Indians to live on reservations. The government encouraged settlers to farm the fertile land. By the 1920s, farming in the Great Plains was booming. A few years of heavy rainfall produced huge yields of wheat and other crops. Owners of large farms got rich.

Turn the page.

People swarmed the streets near the New York Stock Exchange on October 29, 1929.

Then two things happened that helped create a disaster. In 1929, the stock market crashed. People had been buying shares of companies on the stock market to make money. Prices of stocks kept going higher. Some people made a lot of money.

But on Tuesday, October 29, stock market prices fell about 80 percent. People panicked and tried to sell their shares. The stock market crash caused many companies and banks to go out of business. People were left with no money and no jobs. Crop prices fell. People called it the Great Depression.

In 1931, the second part of the disaster began. Rainfall sharply decreased in parts of the Great Plains. The Plains had experienced droughts before, but the rains had always returned. Not this time. Hot winds blew across the land, taking millions of tons of soil with it.

The southern Great Plains, including parts of Oklahoma, Texas, New Mexico, Kansas, and Colorado, dried up and blew away. A reporter calls the area the Dust Bowl, and the name sticks.

Turn the page.

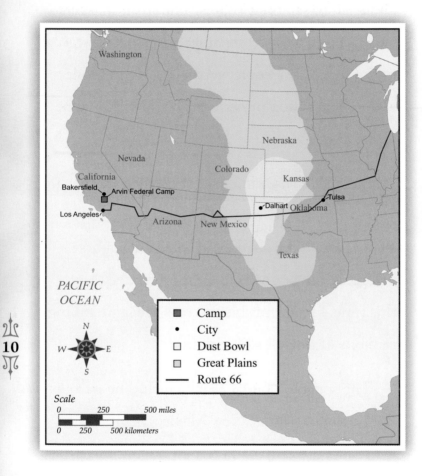

You and millions of other people are living with the horror of the Dust Bowl. Some are determined to stay on their farms. Many give up and move to large cities or to California to start a new life. Others travel to the Dust Bowl to write stories and take photos for the rest of the world to see.

➤To try to stay on your farm, turn to page **13**.

➤To leave your farm to find work elsewhere, turn to page **43**.

➤To be a government photographer in the Dust Bowl, turn to page **73**.

A combination of drought and insects killed crops in the Dust Bowl.

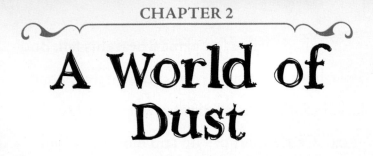

CHAPTER 2

A World of Dust

You stand on the porch of your white clapboard house and look out onto the Kansas land. Farm life is all you've ever known. Three years ago, in 1929, you married your girlfriend, Nettie. Your daughter, Ruby, was born the next year. Your father gave you enough land to start a farm of your own.

Last year, 1931, a drought caused crop failures in other parts of Kansas. But it's not just the drought that has you worried. The crash of 1929 hurt everyone. You took your savings out of the bank before it closed. The money is hidden under a loose floorboard in the kitchen.

Turn the page.

You had planned to plant wheat this fall. But a neighbor tells you to raise cattle instead. Your farm includes grassy pastures where cattle can graze. "Cattle won't dry up and blow away," your neighbor says, laughing.

➤*To plant wheat, go to page* **15**.

➤*To buy cattle, turn to page* **23**.

Last year was a bumper crop for wheat. You think you can make money with wheat this year too. True, prices did go down a little from last year. But you're sure the drop was temporary. Once the fields are planted, it's time to wait for the rain.

You wait. And wait. The sun beats down onto your fields. The newspaper brings more bad news. Wheat prices continue to fall. Last year's huge wheat crop flooded the market and brought down prices.

One morning, you go to the fields and walk through the drooping wheat. You barely notice as the sky darkens. Then the wind picks up. You see a large, dark cloud coming toward you. It's a dust storm! Should you run for the house or stay where you are?

➤To run, turn to page **16**.

➤To stay in the fields, turn to page **33**.

The black cloud barrels across the fields, making a loud, rushing sound. You run to the house as fast as you can. You get inside just as the storm hits. It's black as night inside the house. You hear Nettie and little Ruby crying. You feel in the darkness until you find the kerosene lamp and light it. The light barely makes a dent in the darkness.

The furious wind rattles the windows and doors. Dust pours through the cracks and fills the air, making you cough. After two hours, the terrible howling wind finally stops. Everything in the house is covered with dirt, including you, Nettie, and Ruby. The grit sticks to the roof of your mouth and between your teeth. In a daze, you open the door and go outside.

The wheat field is gone. Everything is covered with dirt and dust. You and Nettie begin shoveling the dirt out of the house.

Huge clouds of dust rolled through the sky, wiping out the sun.

As you are dumping a bucket of dirt in the ditch, an old truck comes wheezing down the road. You don't recognize the man driving it, but he stops and waves.

"My name is Smith," the man says. "I own the land west of here. I'm going to town to see how others fared. You should come too."

→To go into town, turn to page **18**.

→To stay on the farm, turn to page **20**.

Caddo, Oklahoma, was just one of many bleak Dust Bowl towns.

You get into your old truck and head into town. When the crops were good, the town was a busy place. Now most of the businesses are closed. Wind rattles through broken windows. Tumbleweeds skip down the dusty street.

A small crowd is gathered at the general store. A few people lost cattle in the storm. But several farmers, like you, lost their entire crop.

Smith finds you in the crowd. "Such a shame," he says, shaking his head. Then he clears his throat nervously.

"Terrible thing for a family man such as you," he begins. "Me, I don't even live around here. I just come to the farm a few times a year to check on the crops. I'm a banker from Oklahoma City."

"So you're one of those suitcase farmers," you say scornfully. "You buy up land and then plant as much as you can. But you live so far away that you have to pack a suitcase to visit your farm. You don't love the land. You only want to make money from it."

You turn away, but Smith grabs your arm.

"Don't judge me so fast," he says quickly. "I'm here to make you an offer on your land."

Your first reaction is to refuse Smith's offer. Then you remember the dead, dry fields.

➤To stay on the farm, turn to page **20**.

➤To sell your land, turn to page **31**.

Dust storms piled dirt and sand up to the windows of buildings.

Shaking your head, you return to the farm. It's too late now to replant the wheat crop. Even if you did, the hot, dry wind would kill the wheat before it could grow. You do your best to keep the dairy cow and the chickens alive. Nettie sells eggs, milk, and cheese in town to make a few pennies. She sometimes has to strain the milk several times to remove the dirt.

You tack wet sheets and cloths to the windows and doors. Still, you can't keep the dust out of the house. Nettie keeps the plates and cups upside down on the kitchen table. That way, the insides stay clean until you eat.

By 1936, the fifth year of drought, you're worn out. The farm is little more than a desert. The only things that will grow are tumbleweed plants, which you feed to the starving milk cow.

On September 6, you and Nettie listen to President Franklin D. Roosevelt on the radio. He visited the Dust Bowl not long ago. "I shall never forget the fields of wheat so blasted by heat that they cannot be harvested," he says. Then the president begins talking about the Works Progress Administration (WPA). This government program creates jobs for the unemployed, including farmers.

Turn the page.

"I could get a job," you say. "But some of those WPA jobs are far away. I'd hate to leave you and Ruby here alone."

"We could go on drought relief," Nettie says hesitantly. "We'll be able to get help from the government, and you can stay on the farm."

You were raised not to take handouts from anyone, including the government. You're not happy with either choice, but you know you have to do something. The next morning, you drive into town. On one side of the street is the WPA office. Next door, there is a sign that says, "Relief sign-up."

➸To look for a WPA job, turn to page **34**.

➸To sign up for government relief, turn to page **36**.

Soon your herd of cattle is grazing in the grassy pasture. They are round and healthy. You hope that in a few years, you'll have a large ranch.

Summer wears on, and no rain comes. The grass dries up in the heat. You're forced to buy expensive cattle feed from town. You're sure the drought can't last too much longer, though.

One morning, you are outside when you see a large black cloud rumbling toward you. At first, your heart leaps with excitement. The rains are coming! Then you look more closely. That is not a rain cloud. It is a huge dust cloud! You can smell the dirt and feel the wind of the storm rushing at you. The barn isn't too far away. But Nettie and the baby are in the house. Where do you go?

➤ *To run for the barn, turn to page 24.*

➤ *To run for the house, turn to page 28.*

There's no time to round up the cattle. You barely make it to the barn before the storm hits. Dust pours through cracks in the walls. Soon everything in the barn is covered with dust. From the pasture, you can hear the cattle hacking and snorting in panic.

When the wind finally dies down, you rush to the house. Nettie and Ruby are coughing from the dust but seem OK. Next, you check the pasture. The cattle are gray with dust but alive.

Over the next few months, more dust storms roar across the land. The dirt drifts are so high that soon your house is almost buried. Some days you have to climb through the window to get out. The only thing for your cows to eat is sparse, dirt-covered grass and hay. They grow sickly and thin. You're forced to slaughter some of them. Their stomachs are filled with dirt.

By May 1936, things are looking bleak. There's nothing at all left on the land, not even weeds. You keep losing cattle. The calves that are born are sickly. Many of them die.

One morning, you see an article in the newspaper. "Look here," you say to Nettie. "We can ship our cattle to areas in the middle of the state where there is still grass. They can get fattened up and healthy."

Nettie frowns. "Are you sure it's a good idea?" she says. "How can we be sure that they'll be taken care of there?"

"We sure can't take care of them here," you reply sadly. "They're all going to die if they stay."

→To send the cattle away, turn to page **26**.

→To keep them on the farm, turn to page **39**.

You and several neighbors join together to pay the shipping charges for the cattle. They amount to $46 for your part. When Nettie hears about the cost, she gets angry.

"Forty-six dollars?" she says. "That's almost enough to buy an electric washing machine like the rich people have!"

You try to reason with Nettie. "But if we spend this money now, it's like savings in the bank. The cattle will be healthy, and we'll be able to increase our herd."

Nettie finally agrees to the plan. You send away 50 head of cattle.

In the fall, you go to the train station in town to reclaim your cattle. You are shocked to see their condition. Many of them can barely walk down the ramps. Sending away the cattle was a terrible mistake.

Cattle in the Dust Bowl struggled to find food in the dry pastures.

You spend weeks trying to get the cattle healthy with store-bought feed. The cattle slowly begin to gain weight. But the cost of the feed drains the rest of your money.

Your neighbors who shipped their cattle were just as unlucky. Many of them have sold everything and left. You now have no choice. The farm must be auctioned off.

Turn to page 38.

The storm hits before you get inside. The cloud is so black it blocks out the sun completely. You feel around in the dark, coughing and spitting out mouthfuls of dirt. Finally you stumble onto the porch and crawl into the house. Soon the storm is over. The house is filled with dirt. Nettie is crying, and baby Ruby coughs miserably.

As the months drag on, the dust storms keep coming. The dirt piles up so high that it buries the fences, the farm equipment, and even the house. But what worries you most is little Ruby. She struggles to breathe, and her tiny cough breaks your heart. On clear days she seems fine. But there aren't as many clear days as there used to be. One night, you and Nettie have a talk about Ruby's health.

"We need to take her to the doctor," Nettie says. "I've been giving her sugar with a drop of turpentine. But it's not clearing out her lungs as well as it used to."

"We don't have the money," you tell her. "Our savings are gone, and the doctor in town charges a dollar. We only have 75 cents in the money jar, and we need food. If we don't buy food, we'll starve."

"The cow is still giving milk," Nettie replies. "I can get a quarter from selling milk in town. I'm afraid to wait much longer. She's so tiny, and it's so hard for her to breathe."

→To take Ruby to the doctor now, turn to page **30**.

→To wait to take Ruby to the doctor, turn to page **40**.

Red Cross workers taught women to sew masks to keep out the dust.

"You're right, we need to get Ruby to the doctor," you tell Nettie. You have no idea how you will find money for food. But Ruby's health is more important right now.

At the office, the doctor examines Ruby. "It's the dust pneumonia," he says. "You must get this child away from here, or she will die." Breathing in dirt causes dust pneumonia. Your heart sinks as you realize the only way to save Ruby is to leave the farm forever. Everything must be sold.

Turn to page 38.

Smith is right. Your first responsibility is to your family. When Smith tells you his offer, you gasp.

"That's less than half of what the land is worth," you say, startled.

Smith shrugs. "It isn't worth anything now, is it?" he asks. "What are you going to grow on a pile of dust?"

Grudgingly, you agree to Smith's offer. You spend the next two days loading all your furniture onto your creaky old truck. Nettie cries as she packs up the set of china dishes you received as a wedding gift.

Turn the page.

On the morning of the third day, Smith shows up. You sign some papers, and he hands you an envelope. Your chest tightens as you shove the money in your pocket. You take one last look at the dry, bare land. You can barely remember the lush green fields and blue skies of your childhood. Sadly, you and your family climb into the truck and drive away. Soon the farm, and your old life, disappear behind you.

THE END

To follow another path, turn to page 11.
To read the conclusion, turn to page 103.

There's no time to make it to safety. Dropping to the ground, you cover your head with your hands. Soon the cloud is upon you. The air around you is so dark that it seems like night. Gasping and coughing, you pull your shirt collar over your mouth. A heavy feeling falls over your legs and feet. You realize that dirt is piling over you in drifts.

You struggle to your feet. You stagger forward, eyes tightly closed against the stinging dirt. Then the wind hits you, and you fall again. It seems like time stands still as you lie there. You gasp for breath and wonder if this is your last day on earth. Sadly, it is. You suffocate in the dust storm.

THE END

To follow another path, turn to page 11.
To read the conclusion, turn to page 103.

The WPA gave jobs to about 9 million workers between 1935 and 1943.

A tired-looking man is behind a desk in the WPA office. "I need strong backs to build a new city hall in Colby," he says, shoving some papers toward you. "It pays $43 a month."

"How long will I be gone?" you ask.

"Don't know — probably a few months," the man says. "As long as it takes."

It's not much money, but it will keep Nettie and Ruby fed. And it means you won't have to sell the farm. You sign the papers. The next day, you kiss Nettie and Ruby good-bye. You then get on the bus headed to the WPA camp. As the bus drives away, you watch the little town you've known all your life disappear into the distance. You tell yourself you'll return as soon as you can.

THE END

To follow another path, turn to page 11.
To read the conclusion, turn to page 103.

When you walk into the relief office, you're surprised to see several farmers you know standing in line. A woman explains that everyone will receive emergency supplies and food. She also tells you about the erosion control programs such as contour plowing. Contour plowing forms curving rows in the soil, which are less likely to blow or wash away.

For the next few years, you and Nettie do whatever you can to stay alive and keep the farm. You work on several local relief projects, mainly repairing buildings in town. You use contour plowing to till your fields. You also plant trees on the farm and between the fields. In the future, these shelterbelts will help keep the soil in place.

Shelterbelts protected
fields from wind erosion.

In 1939, a miracle happens — the rains
return. In the spring, you plant seeds you received
through the relief program. As the wheat grows
tall and gentle rains fill the sky, you cry tears of
joy. At last, the worst years of your life are over.

THE END

To follow another path, turn to page 11.
To read the conclusion, turn to page 103.

The day of the auction, a small crowd gathers near your barn. They are mostly friends and neighbors. You're afraid that they will try to make this a "10-cent auction," where no bid will go over a few pennies. Then they will sell everything back to you for the money they paid for it. But you don't have the money to buy back anything. You just want this to be over. You ask everyone to let the auction happen normally. They want to help you, so they agree. Everything is sold quickly, mostly to owners of large farms.

When it is over, you climb into your old truck where Nettie and Ruby are waiting. Maybe you'll go to Washington or California — somewhere where the dust doesn't kill everything. You drive away, not looking back.

THE END

To follow another path, turn to page 11.
To read the conclusion, turn to page 103.

You decide to keep your cattle. But one by one, the cattle die. Soon they will all be gone.

One hot day, a stranger arrives. "I'm from the Drought Relief Service," he tells you. "The government will buy your cattle. We pay anywhere from $14 to $20 per animal, depending on its condition. We give the meat to the poor."

You agree to sell your cattle. "You're lucky," the man says as he hands you the cash. "All of your animals are well enough to sell. Most cattle are so sick that we have to shoot them on the spot."

You and Nettie agree to use the government money to move to Kansas City. A few days later, you and your family drive away. You leave the farm to be buried in drifts of dry, brown dirt.

THE END

To follow another path, turn to page 11.
To read the conclusion, turn to page 103.

"Keeping all of us alive is more important," you insist. Nettie nods and comforts Ruby, who is coughing again. The money buys your family enough beans and bread to live on. You're thankful that your family isn't starving. So many farm families are much worse off.

Two weeks pass. Nettie continues to try home remedies on Ruby, including rubbing her chest with a mixture of lard and kerosene.

Early one morning, Nettie goes to Ruby's room to check on her. Suddenly, Nettie's screams echo through the house.

You race into Ruby's bedroom. The baby is lying lifeless in her crib. You gather her limp body to your chest and sob. Nettie collapses on the floor beside you.

A few days later, you and Nettie stand in the town cemetery, along with your family and friends. It breaks your heart to see Ruby's tiny grave. This hateful dust, you think. How many more innocent people will it kill before it's over?

After the funeral, you and Nettie climb into the truck. You've decided to leave Kansas. There's nothing left for you here. The farm is gone. Ruby is gone. The dust has beaten you. You drive away slowly, never looking back.

THE END

To follow another path, turn to page 11.
To read the conclusion, turn to page 103.

People in the Dust Bowl had little food except for what they managed to grow.

CHAPTER 3

Migrants on the Move

Your family's farm in the Oklahoma Panhandle was once rich and productive. Back in the 1920s, your father took out bank loans to build a new barn and buy a new tractor. Then the dust storms came, and the land dried up.

Mother began doing laundry for other people and selling milk and eggs in town. Dad sold the farm equipment. You and your younger brother, Johnny, do extra chores for your neighbors in exchange for food. But it isn't enough to pay off the loans or to keep you from going hungry.

One day Dad comes in from town. "We can't pay our loans, so the bank is taking the farm," he says sadly. "We have to leave."

Turn the page.

"Where are we going?" you ask.

"Well, we could go to Aunt Sally's in Tulsa," Dad replies slowly. "She's offered us a place to stay. But lots of folks are going to California." Dad looks at you. "Where would you like to go?"

→To go to Tulsa, go to page **45**.

→To go to California, turn to page **50**.

"Let's go to Tulsa," you say. "At least there, we'll have Aunt Sally." Your mother agrees.

"Tulsa it is, then," Dad says. You feel sad about leaving the farm, but you're also excited. Tulsa is about 200 miles east of your farm. It takes your old truck most of the day to get there.

It's the biggest city you've ever seen! The streets are filled with cars, buses, and streetcars. The 11th Street Bridge stretches over the Arkansas River. Beside the bridge, hundreds of homeless people live in ramshackle shanties. Dad tells you this slum is called a "Hooverville," after former President Herbert Hoover. Hoover was president during the beginning of the Great Depression. Many people think he didn't do enough to help them. You turn away, glad that you're going to a real house.

Turn the page.

Once you're settled in at Aunt Sally's, Dad starts looking for work. Over the next few weeks, you and Mother help Aunt Sally with the sewing she does for money.

Dad finds a few odd jobs here and there. The sewing doesn't bring in enough money to feed everyone. Dad sells the truck, but it's not enough. Six months after you arrive, Aunt Sally and your parents have a talk.

"I can't do it anymore," Sally says tearfully. "You're my family, and I love you, but there's no money. I don't know what to do."

Dad looks defeated. Mother is crying. "We understand, Sally," Dad says. "We can't ask you to take care of us any longer."

→To move to the Hooverville, go to page 47.

→To leave town, turn to page 64.

Mays Avenue Camp was a Hooverville in Oklahoma City, Oklahoma.

Your heart sinks as you stare at the crowded Hooverville. You and Johnny search for scraps of wood and metal. Dad uses them to make a tiny hut that rattles in the wind. The only place to wash is a dirty drainage ditch.

There are no jobs. Every day, the family lines up at the soup kitchen downtown. At first, you are ashamed to stand in that line. But your hunger makes you lose your shame. You long to leave. But the truck is gone, and there's no money.

Turn the page.

One evening, Dad doesn't come back from looking for work in town. You're not worried. Maybe he found a night job somewhere. Days pass, and he still doesn't return. You're afraid something has happened to him. Then you realize that his clothes are gone as well. He isn't coming back. Mother gathers you and Johnny to her. "It's just us now," she says in a dull voice. "We've got to take care of each other."

You square your shoulders. "I'll go out and find a job," you say, but you're trembling.

Mother hugs you, tears wetting her cheeks. "Bless you," she tells you.

The next morning, you scrub up as best you can and go into the city. The crowds jostle you. The sounds of honking cars fill the air. As you walk down a side street, you pass an old woman huddled on the sidewalk. She grabs your sleeve.

"Please, can you spare a dime?" she asks you.

"I'm sorry, I don't have any money," you say quickly, as you try to pull away from her. She tightens her grip on your arm. "Please," she rasps. "I'm so hungry."

You pull away and run as fast as you can down the street. The shouts of the woman follow you, but she doesn't try to catch you. All you want to do is go back to the shanty, as much as you hate it.

→To return to the shanty, turn to page **60**.

→To keep looking for a job, turn to page **61**.

Before you know it, the old truck is piled high with clothes, furniture, mattresses, and boxes. The next morning, you and Johnny climb into the back of the truck. Mother gets in front, and Dad starts the truck and drives away. You can't wait to see the ocean and the California orange groves everyone talks about.

Soon the family is headed west on Route 66, the main road to California. The truck passes a large billboard that reads "NO JOBS IN CALIFORNIA. OKIES KEEP OUT."

"What are Okies?" you ask. Mother frowns. "That's the name that folks in California give to people who move out there from the Dust Bowl," she replies. "It's short for 'Oklahoma.' It's not a nice name, but don't you worry about it."

As it gets dark, the truck veers off the road. "Flat tire," Dad says. "We'll camp here tonight."

Dust Bowl farm families loaded up their cars for the move to California.

Mother cooks beans over a campfire. Dad struggles to change the tire while you and Johnny pitch the tent. Soon a man walks up to the campsite. He has a head of curly hair and an old guitar slung over his shoulder.

"I'll give you a hand with your flat tire if I can have a bite to eat," he says. "Or I can help you with that tent." You're wary of strangers, but this man seems nice. What do you do?

➤To refuse the man's help, turn to page 52.

➤To let the man help, turn to page 56.

"No thanks," you reply. The man smiles and continues on his way. After a hot meal of beans and bacon, you and Johnny curl up in the truck. Mother and Dad sleep in the tent. As soon as it is light, Dad finishes changing the tire. You're back on the road to California.

Two days later, you cross the California state line. Dad and Mother decide to celebrate by having lunch at a restaurant. Several other migrant families are in the restaurant. Dad begins chatting with the father of one of the families.

"The San Joaquin Valley is where the work is," the man says. "The big farms are always looking for pickers."

"We were planning on going to Los Angeles," Dad says. He turns to you, Mother, and Johnny. "This decision affects all of us. What do you think we should do?"

Mother thinks there is more opportunity in the San Joaquin Valley.

"Los Angeles! I want to see the ocean!" exclaims Johnny. Dad looks at you. "Guess you're the tiebreaker," he says with a smile. "What do you think we should do?"

➤To go to the San Joaquin Valley, turn to page **54**.

➤To go to Los Angeles, turn to page **59**.

Dust Bowl refugees were tired and hungry when they reached California.

You think hard. Los Angeles sounds exciting. But your family knows farming. "I agree with Mother," you say. Johnny's smile disappears.

Dad smiles. "Don't worry, Johnny-cake," he says. "We'll see the ocean one day, I promise."

After driving through the desert, you arrive at the outskirts of the San Joaquin Valley. You are upset to see a huge sign that says "NO WORK. OKIES GET OUT." Dad keeps driving, but you pass several other signs like it. Finally you see a small sign that reads, "Potato harvesters needed."

The truck bumps down a dirt road. At the end is an enormous field. Many people are already at work. The foreman agrees to hire all four of you. The next day, you use a large metal fork to dig the potatoes out of the ground. You've dug potatoes before, just not this many! But once the potatoes are harvested, the family is out of work again. Dad gathers the family together.

"This isn't what I expected when we came out here," he says. "But we're not starving. There's more work picking fruits and vegetables in the north, if we want it. Or we could go to Los Angeles, like we originally planned. I might be able to find some work there."

You're tired of working in the fields. But you don't know if Dad can find work in Los Angeles.

➧*To go to Los Angeles, turn to page 59.*
➧*To keep working in the fields, turn to page 65.*

55

Woody Guthrie wrote many folk songs about his Dust Bowl experiences.

You tell the man to speak to your father. Dad eyes the curly-haired man. Finally he says, "OK, we could use the help."

"Glad to hear it," the man replies, reaching out to shake Dad's hand. "My name's Woody Guthrie." After Woody and Dad change the tire, you all sit down to a meal of beans and bacon. Woody says he grew up in a small Oklahoma town. He tells you about his own kids back in Pampa, Texas. Later, he sings a song he wrote called "Dust Bowl Blues."

When you wake up the next morning, you don't see Woody. "Where is he?" you ask as you help put the cooking supplies in the truck.

"Gone before dawn," Mother replies. "Nice man. I hope things work out for him."

Soon you arrive at the California state line. Several men with rifles block the road. "What's going on here?" Dad asks as the men walk up to the truck.

"You're an Okie, ain't you?" one large man sneers. "There's no room for any more Okies in California."

"You have no right to keep us out," Dad says angrily. The men grip their rifles and step forward. "We're Los Angeles policemen," they say. "We don't want you dirty Okies in California."

Turn the page.

Your family doesn't have enough money to make the trip home. Many people are camping near the state line. Dad decides to join them.

One of the other campers approaches. "We heard of a camp for migrants near Bakersfield," he says, whispering so the guards won't hear him. "There's work there."

"How are you getting there?" Dad asks. "They won't let us pass into California here."

"Got to go north and then into California on Route 15," the man says. "If you want, come with us. We can share food and gas."

➤To stay at the makeshift camp, turn to page **66**.

➤To try to get to Bakersfield, turn to page **68**.

"I think Los Angeles sounds wonderful," you say. Johnny whoops with joy.

After another day of travel, you finally arrive in Los Angeles. Dad drives straight to the ocean. You stand on the sandy beach with your toes in the cold ocean foam.

You move into a tiny but clean apartment a few miles from the beach. Dad is lucky enough to find work quickly. He joins a crew digging ditches, which pays $3 a day. Mother gets a job cleaning houses. You and Johnny enroll in school.

At first it's hard. The other kids call you "dirty Okie." Slowly, though, you make friends. Soon Dad and Mother will make enough money to buy a real house. Life in California is good.

THE END

To follow another path, turn to page 11.
To read the conclusion, turn to page 103.

You're too scared to keep looking for a job. Back at the shanty, you curl up under the dirty blanket. You're trapped here, with no money and no way out. You know you're letting your family down, but you don't know what else to do. You pray that somehow you'll all be able to survive until the Great Depression is over.

THE END

To follow another path, turn to page 11.
To read the conclusion, turn to page 103.

"You can do this," you tell yourself, pushing aside your fear as best you can. But you're not sure where to start. As you pass a coffee shop, you spy a rumpled newspaper on the counter. It gives you an idea. You go inside and sit on one of the stools. You rustle through the newspaper until you find the help wanted ads.

"What'll you have?" asks a thin, tired-looking woman behind the counter.

"Oh, nothing, thank you," you say as politely as you can. "I'm not hungry." Then your stomach growls and gives you away. The woman's eyes soften. "How long has it been since you've had a proper meal, child?" she asks kindly.

"I had some soup last night," you lie. You gave your bowl of soup to Johnny when Mother wasn't looking.

Turn the page.

The woman looks you over. "Tell you what," she says finally. "The other waitress is out sick, and I'm all by myself here. I'll give you food if you'll help me with some chores."

You can't believe your luck. Soon you're gobbling down a plate of eggs and toast.

"I'm Betty," the woman says. "Me and my husband own this joint. It ain't much, but it pays the bills."

When you finish breakfast, you scrub dishes, sweep the floors, and take out the trash. By late that afternoon, you're exhausted. You haven't worked this hard since you left the farm. But your stomach is full for the first time in weeks.

"You've got a strong back and you work hard," Betty says approvingly. "How would you like a permanent job?"

Many people in the cities depended on free soup kitchens for food.

You nod. "Now, I can't pay you wages," Betty says quickly. "But I can give you decent food every day. I expect you to be here every morning and work as hard as you did today. Agreed?"

"Agreed!" you say. Betty gives you a greasy paper sack filled with leftovers. You clutch it as if it were a treasure. Maybe one day, you'll be able to earn money. But for now, food is enough.

THE END

To follow another path, turn to page 11.
To read the conclusion, turn to page 103.

One night, Dad returns to Sally's house with an old, beat-up car. You don't ask where he got it, and he doesn't tell you. You and your family pack your few belongings and drive out of town.

Every time the money runs out, Dad stops and finds work. You camp in pastures and ditches alongside the road. You and Johnny find scraps of food from restaurant garbage cans.

You finally make it to Washington state. You all find jobs picking apples. As soon as one orchard is done, you move on to the next.

"Don't worry," Dad says to you. "We'll find a place of our own someday." You don't think that day will ever come, though, at least not until the Great Depression and drought are over.

THE END

To follow another path, turn to page 11.
To read the conclusion, turn to page 103.

You don't ever want to be hungry again, so the idea of making money sounds good. Dad agrees. The next day, you pack up and move on. For the rest of the summer, you follow the crops, picking fruit and vegetables. By fall, it's time for cotton to be picked. Cotton pickers make $3 to $4 a day, and all four of you can work. It's backbreaking work, and you hate it. But at the end of the season, the family has a nice bit of money saved.

You live in a small cabin near the cotton fields. The owner lets you stay in the cabin during the winter. It's not much, but it's better than spending the winter in a tent. In the spring, it will be time to move again, following the crops.

You decide you don't mind being a migrant worker. It's not the life you imagined, but it's not bad, either.

THE END

To follow another path, turn to page 11.
To read the conclusion, turn to page 103.

Shabby buildings made up many migrant camps in California.

"These men can't keep us out forever," Dad finally says. "We'll stay here until they let us in."

The camp is dirty and crowded. The only water to drink is from an irrigation ditch along the side of the road. The water smells bad and tastes worse.

Every day more people come, and the guards turn them all away. Some leave, but a lot of them set up camp. Soon there are several hundred people camped here. A rumor in the camp says that the guards will be leaving soon. You hope it's true.

One morning, you wake up feeling dizzy. Your stomach hurts terribly. You have bloody diarrhea, which scares you. Mother is worried. She wraps blankets around you. But there's no medicine, and there's nothing more she can do. One of the old women in the camp takes a look at you.

"Dysentery," the woman says, shaking her head. "Must have gotten sick from the water." That night, you die in your sleep.

THE END

To follow another path, turn to page 11.
To read the conclusion, turn to page 103.

People at Arvin Federal Camp lived in clean tents and small cabins.

It takes you a week to get to Bakersfield. The family you travel with is from Kansas. The Dust Bowl destroyed their farm too.

Finally you reach Arvin Federal Camp on Weedpatch Highway. People call it Weedpatch Camp. The government built the camp just for Bowl refugees. Rows of tidy white tents on platforms fill the camp.

Your family is assigned a tent with its own stove. It costs a dollar a week to live in the camp. Families without money do work around the camp in exchange for their lodging. The DiGiorgio fruit farms are nearby. Your parents get jobs in the fields. You and Johnny go to the local school.

Life in camp is better than anything you remember in Oklahoma. The bathrooms have flush toilets and hot showers. There are dances, potluck dinners, and talent shows. The camp has a library and a medical clinic. Later the camp opens its own school.

One day, you see a man wandering around the camp, writing in a notebook. He sees you and Johnny and smiles. "I'm John Steinbeck," the man says. "I'm writing an article on the camps for *Life* magazine."

Turn the

John Steinbeck wrote *The Grapes of Wrath* based on his interviews at Weedpatch Camp.

Mr. Steinbeck asks you and Johnny about life in camp. He writes as you talk. Soon Dad, Mother, and a few others join you. They tell Mr. Steinbeck all about their lives in Oklahoma.

"Thank you for telling me your stories," he says when everyone is finished. "You know, I just might write a book about the Dust Bowl."

As Mr. Steinbeck leaves, you feel sorry for him. You doubt that anyone will be interested in reading a book about Okies and the Dust Bowl.

As the sun sets, your family returns to your tent for dinner. Dad says that soon the family will make enough money to buy a house and some land. You look forward to living a good life in California.

THE END

To follow another path, turn to page 11.
To read the conclusion, turn to page 103.

Many photographers found jobs
with the U.S. government during
the Great Depression.

CHAPTER 4

Documenting the Dust Bowl

It's 1935, and photography is your life. You grew up in New York City. When you were a kid, your mother gave you a used camera. You quickly learned to take good pictures. By the time you graduated from high school, you had a job at a small newspaper. But you lost your job a few months ago when the paper went out of business.

You hear about one of President Franklin Roosevelt's New Deal programs called the Resettlement Administration. The people who run the program are hiring photographers to take photos around the country. You sell everything you own except your camera and rickety car and drive to Washington, D.C.

73

Turn the pa

Roy Stryker was in charge of the photo department of the Resettlement Administration.

Before you know it, you're standing in front of the man who runs the department. "I'm Roy Stryker," the man says, shaking your hand. "So you want to take photos for me?"

You nod as Stryker flips through your folder of photos. He snaps the folder shut and hands it back to you. "Good work. Right now I need photos of the dust storms in Oklahoma and Texas. I could also use some photos of migrant workers in California. I'll pay you $4 a day. Which assignment do you want?"

➤ To go to the Dust Bowl, go to page 75.

➤ To go to California, turn to page 84.

"I'll go to the Dust Bowl, sir," you tell Stryker.

Stryker explains that you will send all of your film back to the office to be processed. Soon you're on the road, heading west. Every night, you pitch your tent by the side of the road. By early April, you reach the Texas Panhandle. You have never seen anything like the Dust Bowl. You can drive for hours and never see anything green. The towns are little more than ghost towns.

Several dust storms have hit the area, but you haven't seen one yet. On Sunday, April 14, you decide to hire a pilot to take you over some of the drought-stricken areas. He agrees to take you for the price of gas, which is 19 cents a gallon. It's a beautiful spring morning with clear skies. You get some great pictures of the destroyed farmlands. As the plane turns, you see something large on the horizon.

Turn the page.

"What's that?" you yell above the roar of the engine.

"Dust storm," the pilot yells back. "It's bigger than anything I've ever seen. We should get out of its way." You want to get more photos of the storm, but is it worth the risk?

→To tell the pilot to keep flying, go to page 77.

→To tell the pilot to land, turn to page 79.

The Black Sunday dust storm covered eastern Colorado, Kansas, Oklahoma, and Texas.

"Let's get closer!" you yell, thinking of the great pictures you could get. The pilot shakes his head but heads straight for the storm.

Leaning out of the cockpit, you snap picture after picture of the oncoming storm. Suddenly a gust of wind hits the plane. It tips crazily to one side. You drop your camera. It falls, disappearing into the black dust cloud.

The engine begins to sputter. "I've got to make an emergency landing!" the pilot yells. The plane dives and hits the ground with a crash.

Turn the page.

77

When you wake up, you are in a hospital. A smiling nurse is beside your bed. "You're lucky," she says. "You only have a broken leg and some bruises." The pilot is all right too. The next day, you call Stryker and tell him what happened.

"You were in a plane on Black Sunday?" he cries.

"Black Sunday?" you say, confused.

"It was a terrible day," Stryker explains. "Huge dust storms struck areas all over the country, sending dust all the way back to Washington, D.C."

"When you're better, you can come back here," he continues. "Or you can stay out on the road and keep taking photos."

➤To go back out on the road, turn to page **81**.
➤To return to Washington, turn to page **101**.

"I think you're right," you yell. The pilot immediately turns back. The black storm gains on you as you race to the landing strip.

"Hang on!" the pilot yells as he lands the plane with several hard bumps. You scramble out of the plane in time to snap several photos of the storm. Then you dash for a small shed.

The storm hits just as you slam the door. Everything goes black, as if a blanket was thrown over the sun. The shed rattles and groans in the wind. Dust fills the air. You can't see the pilot, even though he is standing right beside you.

The storm finally passes. Coughing, you walk out of the shed. The pilot grins at you. "What did you think of your first dust storm?" he asks.

"That was the most frightening thing I've ever seen," you reply.

Turn the page.

"I'm sure it won't be your only one," the pilot says. "They happen all the time these days."

You got your dust storm photos, but you don't want to leave the area yet. The pilot tells you about a struggling farm family nearby. There's also a small town a few miles west that might be a good place to visit. The pilot says some people are filming a movie there.

➤To find the farm family, go to page **81**.

➤To go to the small town, turn to page **83**.

Dust storms made even simple tasks like building a fence a struggle.

You set out on the road. You come to a row of fence posts almost completely buried in the dirt. A man and his son are trying to dig them out. You ask if you can take their picture. The man agrees and tells you he's a wheat farmer. "But we haven't been able to raise a crop here for three years," he adds.

You follow the man and the boy to a small farmhouse. The windows and doors are covered with wet sheets to keep the dust out. A woman and several ragged children greet you. You take several pictures as the woman tells their story.

Turn the page.

"This place was nice once," she says sadly. "Wheat as far as you could see." She leads you to the back of the house, where a small vegetable garden is growing. To your surprise, the plants are green and healthy.

"We water them by hand every day," the woman says proudly. "We carry water from the well. This garden will keep us fed this year." You don't see how those few plants will feed the family, but you don't say anything.

You thank the family and go on your way. There's a small town nearby where you might get some good photos. Or you could move on to the next county. You've heard about some farm auction sales going on there.

➤ To visit the town, go to page **83**.

➤ To go to the next county, turn to page **94**.

Soon you arrive in Dalhart, Texas. You spend a few days here, taking pictures and talking to the local people.

The big news in town is that a government movie crew is here. They're making a movie about the Dust Bowl called *The Plow That Broke the Plains*. Bam White, a local farmer, is going to be in the movie.

You watch the cameramen film Bam White pretending to plow a field. They pay him $25.

Your assignment is over in a few days. This has been an adventure, but you're tired of being on the road all the time. When you tell Stryker, he begs you not to quit. "I can use you here," he says. "Come back to Washington, D.C."

Turn to page 101.

You've heard stories about Dust Bowl refugees, penniless and homeless, who follow the harvests in California. These migrant workers travel from farm to farm picking crops.

As you make your way across Route 66, you're surprised at the number of people heading west. Old cars and trucks piled high with furniture fill the roads. Every few miles, you see a car broken down beside the road. Usually you stop and take pictures. Each family has a sad story of their Dust Bowl experience. Most of them hope to find a better life in California.

One afternoon, you stop at a gas station and notice a woman with dark hair and rumpled clothing. She's carrying a camera. Her eyes take in everything, and she often lifts the camera to her face and snaps a picture. As it turns out, she's also a government photographer.

In the 1930s, Dorothea Lange was the most famous government photographer.

"I'm Dorothea Lange," she says as you shake her hand. She's returning from the migrant fields in California. "Be careful," she says as she gets back in her car. "It'll tear your heart out, seeing what those people are going through." She wishes you luck and drives away.

Finally you cross the border into California and start to see signs like "pea-pickers' camp," and "migrant camp this way." Which do you follow?

➤To go to the pea-pickers' camp, turn to page 86.

➤To head to the migrant camp, turn to page 90.

Lange's photo "Migrant Mother" showed the world the terrible conditions in the Dust Bowl.

You head down the tiny dirt road to the pea-pickers' camp. At the side of the road is a lone tent, its tattered sides flapping in the breeze. A truck with no tires sits next to the tent.

Inside, a young woman clutches a small baby. Three other children stand near her, staring at you. They are all dirty, with dull eyes. You introduce yourself and ask if you can take their picture. The woman nods, unsmiling.

"Where is everyone?" you ask. "I expected the place to be filled with workers."

"Crops froze," the woman replies. "We're waiting for the next crop to come in. I sold the tires off the truck to buy food, so we're stuck here."

You want to help, but there isn't much you can do. You give each child a penny. They stare at the coins as if they were gold. The mother continues to stare into space. "We're waiting for the next crop to come in," she says again, quietly.

Dorothea was right. It breaks your heart. You can't just leave them there to starve. Maybe you could buy them food. Or you could replace their tires. That might help them move on to find more work.

→To look for tires, turn to page **88**.

→To go to town to buy food, turn to page **96**.

You pull into the first gas station you see. There's a pile of old tires behind the station. A thin young man with greasy fingernails strolls out to greet you.

"How much for the tires back there?" you ask. "I need four of them."

"Quarter apiece," the man replies. "Pick out what you need."

You find four tires that don't look too worn and give the man a dollar. You load the tires into the car and head back to the camp.

The woman looks stunned when you return. "I don't know why you done this, but thank you," the woman says over and over. When you finish putting the tires on her car, you give the family another dollar. "Good luck," you say. You take several pictures of them, and then drive away.

Where will you go now? You remember the signs you passed earlier. One pointed to a migrant camp. You also remember another one that said something about a fruit-pickers' camp.

→To go to the migrant camp, turn to page **90**.

→To go to the fruit-pickers' camp, turn to page **97**.

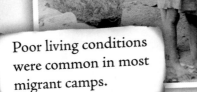

Poor living conditions were common in most migrant camps.

When you reach the migrant camp, you're surprised at the number of people living there. You pitch your own tent and wander through the camp, taking pictures of people as you go.

"What are you all doing here?" you ask a man repairing a broken-down truck.

"We were blown out of Oklahoma," the man says. "We're waiting for the crops to come in so we can pick them."

As you talk, several other men join you. One is a farmer from Kansas who lost his farm when the town's bank closed. Another is a teacher from Oklahoma City. He couldn't find work because no one can afford to pay teachers. He hopes to get a job at the cannery up north when the crops are harvested.

"You might want to talk to the Ritchie family," one man says. "They came all the way from Arkansas, and they've had some hard times."

"There's the Cooks too," another says. "They've got eight young'uns and no mama."

➤*To try to find the Cook family, turn to page 92.*
➤*To look for the Ritchie family, turn to page 99.*

It's easy to find the Cook camp. You simply follow the sounds of many children playing. As you get to their tent, eight dirty, laughing kids surround you. You introduce yourself and take several pictures of the children. They bombard you with questions.

"How do you make pictures?" "Can I make one?" "Where did you come from?" You laugh and let each child hold the camera. Soon a man in weathered overalls strides up.

"Quit pestering!" he shouts, and the children scatter like mice. "I'm Fred Cook," he says.

As you snap pictures, Mr. Cook tells you that his wife died on the trip out to California. Now he's raising all eight children by himself. To your surprise, he doesn't seem bitter.

"It's not so bad, really," he says. "All but little Jim are old enough to work in the fields. After the harvest, I expect we'll go back home to Kansas for the winter. I've got family there, and the kids can go to school."

You thank Mr. Cook for his time and wander through the camp. As you take pictures, you can't help but think about the lives of these people. They come from many places, but they have all ended up here. All because of the dust.

It's time to move on. Where do you go next?

→To head to the fruit-pickers' camp, turn to page **97**.

→To go back to Washington, D.C., turn to page **101**.

You continue on, looking for more people to photograph. The things you see break your heart. In one small town, you attend an auction the farmers call a "10-cent sale." To keep a farmer from losing his property, his neighbors bid pennies on everything. Then they sell everything back to the farmer for the same price, free and clear of the bank.

A thin, stooped man is standing off to the side. A boy about 7 or 8 years old is with him.

"Is this your farm?" you ask.

"Yup," the man replies. "Been here most of my life. My daddy farmed this land. I intend to pass it on to my boy here."

The auction starts. No one bids more than a few cents for any item. When the huge tractor comes up, one man bids 50 cents. The auctioneer shakes his head, but he lets the bid win.

You get some great shots of the auction. After the sale, the bidders crowd around the farmer. The farmer gives them money, and they return the items to him. As you drive away, you see the boy climb onto the tractor, a grin on his face. You know the odds are against the man and his son, but you hope they make it.

In Oklahoma, you photograph relief workers passing out shoes and clothes to the poor. You're tired of grit in your food, of drinking dust-filled water, and seeing the tired, hungry people. It's time to go back to Washington, D.C.

You're angry that the government isn't doing more to help. You hope your pictures will make them realize the terrible toll of the Dust Bowl.

THE END

To follow another path, turn to page 11.
To read the conclusion, turn to page 103.

"Let me see what I can do," you say as you climb back into your car. There's a small town a few miles down the road. You find the tiny grocery store and go inside.

You pile bread, bologna, beans, and peanut butter on the counter. As you pay for the food, you tell the grocer what you're doing.

"You're feeding those dirty Okies?" he spits. "It was a black day when those folks came to California." You take your bag and leave quickly.

Your car bumps back down the road to the camp. The tent and the truck are still there, but the woman and her children are gone. You set the bag of groceries in the tent. The family will see them when they get back. As you drive away, you wonder what will become of them.

THE END

To follow another path, turn to page 11.
To read the conclusion, turn to page 103.

The fruit-pickers' camp is much nicer than some of the other migrant camps you've seen. The owner of the fields has built several rows of tiny but neat cabins along the edge of the field. Clean laundry hangs on several clotheslines, snapping in the breeze. A few children play around the cabin doorsteps as a group of women watch them.

You strike up a conversation with the women. They are happy to let you take pictures and tell you about the camp.

"We take turns watching the young'uns," one young mother says. "That way, all of us can work some days and make money."

"The owner is good to us," another says. "We come here from Arizona every summer to work. Once the harvest is over, we go back home. We've been doing that for a few years now."

Turn the page.

They tell you about life in the camp. The grower owns several large operations, so there is plenty of work. There is a school where the older children go when they're not in the fields. Sometimes there is a dance or other entertainment. Once a week, a bus comes to take people to town.

"It's a sight better than Kansas," one woman says, tears in her eyes. "The dust killed two of my babies. They came down with dust pneumonia and died on the same day. I'd rather live in a tent here than in my own house in the Dust Bowl."

Your assignment in California is almost over. The pictures you took are back in Washington, and you hope they do some good. Maybe it's time you headed back to Washington too.

Turn to page **101**.

Many people escaped the Dust Bowl by moving to camps in California.

You find the Ritchie family at the edge of camp, near a smelly ditch. A woman in a tattered dress is washing dishes in the brown ditch water. A baby sleeps on an old quilt on the ground.

You introduce yourself and take a few pictures. The woman points to the quilt on the ground. "I made that myself," she says proudly. "It was the one thing I couldn't leave behind when we left our farm in Arkansas."

Turn the page.

"Was it bad there?" you ask.

The woman doesn't answer for a moment. Then she says, "I lost my baby girl, Ethel, to the dust pneumonia. This one was born after we got here last fall." She smiles and strokes the baby's head. "He won't ever have to breathe that terrible dust."

You thank her and go on your way. After walking around a bit more, you decide to stay a while. Over the next few days, you take hundreds of pictures. You photograph the outhouses, the tents, and the people. Day by day, families begin to leave, following the ripening crops. Soon it's your turn to leave too. But you'll never forget the migrant camps and the people you met there.

THE END

To follow another path, turn to page 11.
To read the conclusion, turn to page 103.

100

When you get back to Washington,
Mr. Stryker gives you a job cataloging and
recording all of the photos that the other
Resettlement Administration photographers
send in. It's steady work, and you're grateful for it.
Someday you might go back out on the road.
But for now, you're content to stay in the city.

THE END

To follow another path, turn to page 11.
To read the conclusion, turn to page 103.

Today, much of the land in the Dust Bowl has returned to native grasses.

CHAPTER 5

The Legacy of the Dust Bowl

The Dust Bowl lasted from 1931 to 1939. During that time, millions of people lost their homes and jobs. Thousands died.

At first, no one understood why the Dust Bowl happened. After a while, people figured out that they were partly to blame. Bad farming practices left millions of acres of land open to erosion. Land that was not meant for farming was stripped of its grass, which held the soil in place. When the droughts came, the land dried up and blew away.

As the drought continued, the government urged farmers to learn ways to conserve the land. Farmers planted trees and plowed fields in contoured rows. When the rains came in 1939, the Dust Bowl years ended.

In 1941, the United States' entry into World War II (1939–1945) helped end the Great Depression. The war created millions of jobs, and the economy recovered.

The people who lived through the Dust Bowl years never forgot them. Most of the families who left the Dust Bowl never returned. However, not everyone was destroyed by the Dust Bowl. Many families stayed on their farms. When the drought was over, they began farming again. Today there are many successful farms in the area that was once the Dust Bowl.

Some people became famous as a result of their Dust Bowl and Great Depression experiences. Woody Guthrie's songs about life during the Depression made him a star. Dorothea Lange's photographs showed people the horrors of the Dust Bowl. Her photo "Migrant Mother" is one of the most famous pictures in the world. In 1939, John Steinbeck published his book about the Dust Bowl, *The Grapes of Wrath*. It was based on his interviews with people who fled the Dust Bowl for California. The book won the Pulitzer Prize and is still popular today.

During the Dust Bowl years, the government bought millions of acres of land that could not grow crops. Much of this land became parks and national grasslands where the natural vegetation was allowed to grow. Today visitors can see what the Great Plains looked like before the dry, terrible Dust Bowl years.

Time Line

October 29, 1929 — On "Black Tuesday," the stock market crashes. The Great Depression begins.

1931 — Severe drought hits the Midwest. Crops die. "Black blizzards," or dust storms, begin.

1932 — Fourteen dust storms are reported; Franklin D. Roosevelt is elected President of the United States.

1933 — Many of President Roosevelt's "New Deal" programs begin, such as the Agricultural Adjustment Administration.

1934 — The drought worsens and covers more than 75 percent of the United States.

1935 — The government creates the Drought Relief Service to help Dust Bowl families.

The new Soil Conservation Service starts teaching farmers ways to control soil erosion.

The Resettlement Administration begins hiring photographers to document the effects of the Dust Bowl.

On Sunday, April 14, the worst dust storm of the Dust Bowl hits several states and carries dust to the East Coast. People call it "Black Sunday."

1935 — The new Works Progress Administration provides jobs to unemployed Americans.

1936 — Roosevelt is reelected president; Los Angeles sends policemen to patrol the California borders.

1937 — The Resettlement Administration becomes the Farm Security Administration.

1938 — Government conservation programs help keep 65 percent of the soil from blowing away.

1939 — Rains come during the fall, ending the drought; John Steinbeck publishes *The Grapes of Wrath* about the Dust Bowl.

1941 — The United States enters World War II, which helps end the Great Depression.

OTHER PATHS TO EXPLORE

In this book, you've seen how the events surrounding the Dust Bowl look different from three points of view.

Perspectives on history are as varied as the people who lived it. You can explore other paths on your own to learn more about what happened. Seeing history from many points of view is an important part of understanding it.

Here are some ideas for other Dust Bowl points of view to explore:

+ Not all people in the Dust Bowl lost their money. What would it be like to be a wealthy person during that time?

+ The Dust Bowl affected more people than just farmers. What would it be like to be a business or bank owner during the Dust Bowl?

+ Many teenagers went out on their own during the Dust Bowl. What would their lives have been like?

READ MORE

Heinrichs, Ann. *The Dust Bowl.* Minneapolis: Compass Point Books, 2005.

Levey, Richard H. *Dust Bowl!: The 1930s Black Blizzards.* New York: Bearport, 2005.

Reis, Ronald A. *The Dust Bowl.* New York: Chelsea House, 2008.

Vander Hook, Sue. *The Dust Bowl.* Edina, Minn.: Abdo, 2009.

INTERNET SITES

FactHound offers a safe, fun way to find educator-approved Internet sites related to this book.

Here's what you do:

1. Visit *www.facthound.com*
2. Choose your grade level.
3. Begin your search.

This book's ID number is 9781429623438.

FactHound will fetch the best sites for you!

Glossary

auction (AWK-shuhn) — a sale where goods are sold to the person who bids the most money

drought (DROUT) — a long period of weather with little or no rainfall

dust pneumonia (DUHST noo-MOH-nyuh) — a serious sickness caused by breathing dust

dysentery (DI-sen-tayr-ee) — a serious infection of the intestines that can be deadly; dysentery is often caused by drinking contaminated water.

migrant (MYE-gruhnt) — a laborer who moves from place to place

Okie (OAK-ee) — a negative term for a migrant farm worker from the Dust Bowl

relief (ri-LEEF) — money or other help given to poor people

stock market (STOK MAR-kit) — a place where stocks are bought and sold; someone who owns a share of stock owns part of a company.

suffocate (SUHF-uh-kate) — to die from lack of oxygen

BIBLIOGRAPHY

American Experience — Surviving the Dust Bowl
http://www.pbs.org/wgbh/amex/dustbowl/filmmore/
transcript/transcript1.html

Dust Bowl Migration Digital Archives
http://www.csub.edu/library/special/dustbowl/dustbowl.
shtml

Egan, Timothy. *The Worst Hard Time: The Untold Story
of Those Who Survived the Great American Dust Bowl.*
Boston: Houghton Mifflin, 2006.

Gregory, James N. *American Exodus: The Dust Bowl
Migration and Okie Culture in California.* New York:
Oxford University Press, 1989.

Library of Congress: Voices from the Dust Bowl
http://lcweb2.loc.gov/ammem/afctshtml/tshome.html

Stein, Walter J. *California and the Dust Bowl Migration.*
Westport, Conn.: Greenwood Press, 1973.

Worster, Donald. *Dust Bowl: The Southern Plains in the
1930s.* New York: Oxford University Press, 1979.

**Wunder, John R., Frances W. Kaye, and Vernon
Carstensen, eds.** *Americans View Their Dust
Bowl Experience.* Niwot, Colo.: University Press of
Colorado, 1999.

INDEX